a little girl name destiny who loves to pray

Bren Daniels

A LITTLE GIRL NAME DESTINY WHO LOVES TO PRAY

iUniverse books may be ordered through booksellers or by contacting:

iUniverse LLC
1663 Liberty Drive
Bloomington, IN 47403
www.iuniverse.com
1-800-Authors (1-800-288-4677)

ISBN: 978-1-4917-4009-5 (sc)
ISBN: 978-1-4917-4011-8 (hc)
ISBN: 978-1-4917-4010-1 (e)

Library of Congress Control Number: 2014912559

Printed in the United States of America.

iUniverse rev. date: 08/01/2014

I dedicate this book to Destiny Hamilton. I will always remember how she loved to pray. How she could walk in the room, she lifted me up when I was down. I thank God for giving her to me. God would put words in her mouth to say to me countless times, that would take away my sadness. She could make me smile sometimes. I even took her advice even being a little girl. She was always a wise child very peculiar. I know God has a call on her life to preach his word. I know she is chosen by God. I love her dearly she will always be my little girl, who I know loves to pray. She will always be very special to me. Thank you Jesus for giving her to me.

introduction

In our world children need guidance and they want guidance. Destiny is a little girl who is very excited about seing God answer her prayers when she pray.

This book is about prayer. Teaching your children how to pray and to have a love for God.

My mom taught me how to pray.

— mom and I praying

Bren Daniels

My name is Destiny and I am 5 years old. And I love to pray.

Bren Daniels

Mom let's make a circle and pray.

– my mom and my sister and I praying

My mom would teach my sister and I scriptures. And we knew 5 scriptures. And she could call them out and mix them up and we knew them.

She would say.
Say Ephesians 5:1 Be ye therefore followers of God as dear children.

mom teaching my sister and I scriptures

Then she would say. Say Philippians 4:13 I can do all things through Christ which strengtheneth me.

Then she would say. Say I Peter 5:7 Casting all your care upon him; for he careth for you.
Then she would say. Say Psalm 100:1 Make a joyful noise unto the Lord, all ye lands.
Then she would say. Say Matthew 6:9

Our Father which art in heaven. Hallowed be thy name. Thy kingdom come. Thy will be done in earth, as it is in heaven. Give us this day our daily bread. And forgive us, our debt, as we forgive our debtors, And lead us not into temptation, but deliver us from evil: For thine is the kingdom, and the power, and the glory, forever. A-men.

I love for my mom to lay hands on me and lay me back on the floor when praying for me.

Destiny falling back when praying for her

When my mom call my grandma. When she prays for her on the phone. I also like to pray for her.

I love to pray for my mom. I even want her to fall back on the floor when I pray for her.

I love to pray at Church when we have Youth Prayer Night.

Standing in front of Church praying with other kids. — We have to stand in line to wait our turn.

Bren Daniels

When I go to school in the morning. I love for my mom to pray for me before leaving the house to get on the bus.

I was at school one day and my mom forgot my sunflower seeds for a project I needed that day. So I put my head on the desk and prayed to God that she would bring them and she did. And later on that day when she came to pick me up from school. On our way home. I asked her you know why you brought me them sunflower seeds? I told her because I put my head on the desk and prayed to God that's why you brought them.

My mom was in the kitchen one day and I was in my bedroom praying. I was trying to mark her praying in tongues. So she heard me and came into the room and hugged me. She thought that was so cute me marking her.

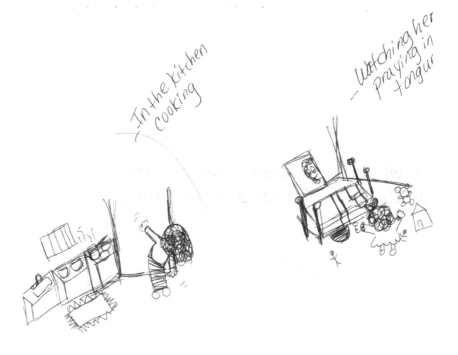

In the kitchen cooking

Watching her praying in tongue

Bren Daniels

And when I go to bed at night. I love to pray to God to thank him for a great family.

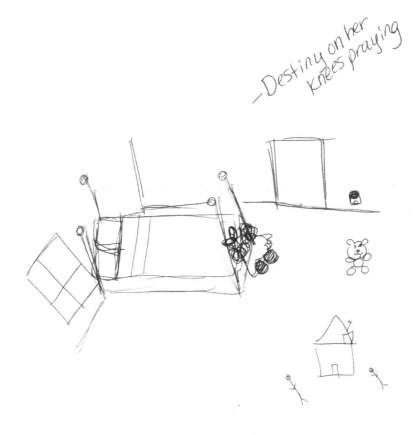

_Destiny on her knees praying

One day my mom was sitting on the sofa in the living room.

My Mom was sad.

I went up to her and prayed for her.

Destiny praying for mom

I said I buke you devil loose Bren.

Immediately my mom start feeling better, she laughed at me.

In the summer my sister and I would go stay with my grandma sometimes.

One day my aunt tooth was hurting when she was at my grandma house.

I asked her could I pray for her.

My aunt let me pray for her.

I laid my hand on her head.

I prayed for her.

I said I pray for your tooth to stop hurting. In Jesus name I pray Amen.

My aunt tooth stop hurting.

Thank you Jesus.

While we were at my grandma house in the summer.

My mom would tell my grandma to call the same scriptures out to us, the ones she called out to us at night.

She didn't want us to forget them over the summer.

My grandma would call them out to us.

Ephesians 5:1

Be therefore followers of God as dear children.

Philippians 4:13

I can do all things through Christ which strengtheneth me.

I Peter 5:7

Casting all your care upon him; for he careth for you.

Psalm 100:1

Make a joyful noise unto the Lord, all ye lands.

Matthew 6:9

Our Father which art in heaven.

Hallowed be thy name. Thy kingdom come.

Thy will be done in earth, as it is in heaven.

Give us this day our daily bread.

And forgive us, our debts, as we forgive our debtors.

And lead us not into temptation, but deliver us from evil:

For thine is the kingdom, and the power, and the glory, forever. A-men.

My grandma would call them out to us before going to bed at night.

I would always see my mom praying over the house every night before going to bed.

I would follow her why she prayed over our house.

My mom would go to the back door and release angels to protect us at night why we sleep.

My mom would go to the other back doors. We had two back doors.

Mom and
Destiny
↖ at
other
back
door.

My mom would go to the side door and pray.

mom at
side
door
Destiny
with
her

My mom would go to the front door and pray.

Destiny
following
mom

Bren Daniels

She would always release **angels** all around our house to protect us while we sleep.

pictures
of
angels

My mom would do that every night before going to bed.

I would always see my mom in her room praying in the morning.

mom praying in the morning

I would see my mom praying at night.

mom praying at night

When I see my mom praying it makes me want to pray.

I just love to pray. Praying is what I love to do.

I just love to pray,pray,pray.

picture
of
Destiny
praying

Bren Daniels

My mom had a headache one day.

My mom asked me to pray for her.

When I pray for my mom she felt better.

When I go to bed at night I love to pray to God, to thank him for a great family.

Destiny on her knees praying

When you know your child loves to pray, encourage them to pray. You never know how God is going to use them one day. They may preach the word of God. They may even intercede in prayer for others. You never know so support them and be glad for them. God has given them a desire to pray to him. I was inspired by God to write this book, because when my little girl was 5 years old. She loved to pray. And I enjoyed her praying to God. I taught my little girls how to pray at a young age. They would bless me when I see them praying. These are true events that happen when she was at the age of 5 years old. Teach your children to fear the Lord at a young age. So they will be careful what they do in life, knowing that God is watching them. Bring them up in the nurture and admonition of the Lord. The Bible says Train up a child in the way he should go. And when he is old he will not depart from it. And even if they depart you have planted the seed inside of them and they will one day come back to the Lord. Proverbs 22:6 You put it in them God knows when to bring it out of them.

By: Bren Daniels
Jesus The Writer

Bring them up in the fear of the
Lord. In Jesus name. Amen